SYNTHETIC
JUNGLE

ALSO BY MICHAEL CHANG

DRAKKAR NOIR

CHINATOWN ROMEO

BOYFRIEND PERSPECTIVE

ALMANAC OF USELESS TALENTS

SYNTHETIC JUNGLE

POEMS

MICHAEL CHANG

Curbstone Books / Northwestern University Press
Evanston, Illinois

Curbstone Books
Northwestern University Press
www.nupress.northwestern.edu

Printed in the United States of America

10   9   8   7   6   5   4   3   2   1

Library of Congress Cataloging-in-Publication Data

Names: Chang, Michael (Poet), author.
Title: Synthetic jungle : poems / Michael Chang.
Description: Evanston : Curbstone Books/Northwestern University Press, 2023.
Identifiers: LCCN 2022049982 | ISBN 9780810146211 (paperback) |
    ISBN 9780810146228 (ebook)
Subjects: BISAC: POETRY / American / General | POETRY / LGBTQ |
    LCGFT: Poetry.
Classification: LCC PS3603.H35736 S96 2023 | DDC 811.6—dc23/eng/20221014
LC record available at https://lccn.loc.gov/2022049982

CONTENTS

SYNTHETIC
JUNGLE

CHARM AGAINST TOO MANY APPLES

honey-pink

~

green-pink

~

cream-green

~

green-blue

~

red-brown

~

reddish-gold

~

brown-gray

~

gray-white

~

black-white, swallowing everything

~

chicken & duck nipple talk, ur kate beckett to my richard castle

~

orogeny of passion, launched from longing to longing

~

all these articles abt happiness make me unhappy

CADUCITY

the syphilitic priest

----

that creep malcolm gladwell

----

the decimating, ravishing, absolutely unwavering straightness of a hemsworth

----

rukeyser's cry for "no more masks!" not aging well

----

resenting poems that tell me what to do ("no offense" to caconrad, koestenbaum . . .)
(hating direction although i am a chinese)

----

asking the difficult questions as a poet: charlie puth or shawn mendes?

----

bunny with 3 ears listening extra close

----

fist-fucked by anwar hadid while he mutters gibberish

----

he looks dazed, collapsible

----

watching u smoke & drink everything in sight

----

trimming ur nose hairs in advance of our date

----

falling asleep on the toilet, bowels exposed

----

spotlighting u, putting u on a pedestal, an ode to the *too much*

----

the impulses we failed to adequately heed (or heeded too well)

----

training myself, some unquestionable authority

----

dreaming of love (meaning erotic potential)

----

processing cum like a college drain

----

comparing things to bullets, american sniper

----

r u straight or complicated

----

governed by wish or propelled by aspiration

----

our season, perfect

----

i can feel another poem coming

MOTIVATIONAL SPEAKER WITH NO MOTIVATION

the best-kept secret

the hole-in-the-wall chicken shop

the most successful surgery

i need a throne for my big chinese brain

an ottoman for my flawless cantonese

a stool for my half-assed poetry

take off ur pants before u fart

all u ever do is fade away

everything good is above the surface

the ugly feelings i've hidden in the wine locker

all the way to the ground

the little gods we fear, so petty

for u i'll be the softest mattress

the fairest ref

the showbiz family of circus lions

happy animals singing

at the altar

a thousand lamps

the motel, forever shut

the beavers, i said

it gets lonely at the top

YOUR PLACE, OR ANOTHER TRIP TO DEAN & DELUCA

the reason white ppl can immediately recall instances of "reverse racism" is b/c such incidents are few & far between . . . i was once told abt a supposedly jarring incident from b4 i was born & pretended to be appropriately aghast

i moved last thursday b/c it was storming & have been in a haze ever since & having nearly gotten over my horrible compulsion to drop things into the deep fryer, spent, really, an inordinate amount of time, like a slow rain, lost in ur hair, then ur neck, circling the rim of desire, a feeling so total & insistent it must've been what the cool kids call "edging"

guys always want u to take their load but have they ever stopped to consider (!!!) what a heavy burden it is to carry

as if i needed to be reminded of his tousled hair & easy grace, they admired his monied garb & accoutrements: gray suit, sensible tie, loafers polished to a shine, fine gold watch (patek), sunglasses (gold frame/yellow lenses, tom ford), he came to_ abruptly

i hadn't heard "friend of dorothy" in a while, used "pulpy" to mean extraneous b/c i only drink juice w/o, green card lottery . . . prized complicity . . . wut can we do ???

u recognize the voice, no, the scent, of someone who wronged u, no, someone who was there when u needed them, a good samaritan, & u jerk ur head back, but it's too late, he's boarding, u give chase

this is my polemic reaching out hoping to encounter another, an effort to arrive at more love, i do romance the only way i know how, pastasciutta, frutti di mare, colors devouring us garden-like, last text: "u know who else was vegetarian!"

there are two places the phrase "my friend" is particularly pernicious: the back of a cab & the floor of the united states senate . . . like haha my friend the pederast i like those old-school eye-talian places that get u a glass of wine while u wait for ur fifth night of takeout in a row

is there anything more refreshing than chilled watermelon & aperol spritzes by the pool in a city of bronze gods is there anything more elegant than champagne & tiny bowls of little glazed fruit hand-picked by the savviest of peasants (i am joking, leave me to my agony)

i want to stare at u till my eyes fall out, i've stopped looking for signs, left the table, refused to participate, am no longer interested in responsibility

take care of urself, that alluring triangle of ur sex, don't let anyone extinguish ur light, tho death is not final, death is a promise, a new beginning, i want the name recognition of princess di the shamelessness of tonya harding the tenacity of genghis khan let us join in dialogue w/ the infinite

like jesus said, i am thirsty . . . ur place, or another trip to dean & deluca (???) hmu

SINGLES' NIGHT AT THE MUSEUM

no matter my efforts to nudge u toward humanity

u hold me down

use ur reproductives

screw me sideways to lana del rey

blow my back out

make me *really* feel it like JFK

when u asked if i could handle it

i thought u meant the stress of being a rockstar poet

but of coz u meant ur dick

gripping it thru ur navy cords

u said *no one is getting this bitch!*

then called me a slur for another race

it was a very confusing 24 hours

but (bitch!) i'm urs

SUPPOSEDLY A MORNING PERSON

想念你的每个角度

i see how they look at you, then at me

how they look at us

are we what they see—imagine

don't answer—lemme bundle it with an energy drink

what abt a marihuana-scented candle

somehow you made "no" feel like "not right now"

freaky, freaky, your bitches steady

you said *this is one of your more vulnerable poems*

i said yea, cuz of you, you made me this way

burned all my yearbooks cuz boring is worse than fake

why'd you say that i'm not responsible for how you feel—

& you're not responsible for how i feel

where does that leave us

parking lot at little caesars

deep love, bargain prices

app says our order's in the river

you'll be the one getting wet

you keep telling ppl they matter, but you matter the most

you can gloat, didn't need to say you wouldn't be jealous

duh, you're not even into me

your toothbrush needs a charge

come collect it, baby

WHITE FORD BRONCO

the vampire technician will only enter if invited

like us, nowhere to go but up

fat wit boredom

i love to be disappointed by alex dimitrov

maltese chick says *let the man walk*

good advice if i ever heard it

how are your fuccboi sonnets

in this timeline you aren't cruel

tight like boy from amherst

i'm a hysterical chinese

a singular thought crowding out all others

piping music into me

flatter me wit your tight lips

wrap them tighter

tighter

chaos butter

yogurty hunk

a fine schmear

can you ever trust

hearts for eyes

shoulder killing me

you are forever

SOUTHPAW

My favorite chef, Kim Gordon

Slow bonds

The (loose needs of) other boys

Breath-reeking, cock-waving

masses of hair

Great heaving meat

Climb in boy like back seat

Rattle rattle in my chest

The animals move together

U crawl like beetle

I go on worshipping

Hands, mouth, wherever

POLAR BEARS IN LITTLE ITALY

---

* i hate linen it's so wobbly & indecisive & lacking in substance like zayn's foreskin breakfast alone i've never had a better burrito my thought pollution wild untouchable cute tender whiteboys rarely disappointed (disappointing?) u say they look the same but i can tell the difference it takes an education no outrage our softest reasoning my heart rate increasing when u put a powerful thing next to something small unpredictable the way flames leap more than memory my hands impatient all trunk no splinter & the suction CONTAINS TUNA. when i was clerking in memphis i never stopped laughing at the way southern lawyers say *voir dire* boldly go where no chinese has gone before at starbux say *call me by ur name* mistake me for someone less famous lines like guppies poems lumpy potato pierogi parnassus is in north jersey rite shop at macy's once a decade but i'm not a schmuck rather a speaker of debasement & terror anyway what choice is there lemon peppa ur a landmark a shiny wonder halo to praise these little comets how they hate what they see & melt crucial things through lime our to odd & splendid wouldn't u say . . .

BEST BUDDIES, 1990

Every day I walk past the mattress store & spot the guy who sold me my mattress. He looks at me like he knows how I sleep, like he has watched me snooze

You cradle your pigeon, insisting it is a peregrine falcon

You're a going-places boy. Gaunt & gallant, nice haircut & a best friend you'd die for

Holding hands, hardly talking, sipping tequila in the quiet. Boy you sank my battleship

It's hard when in my field of vision there's only you—but in your field of vision there's this person & that person & those ppl & the girl at the bar & maybe—only if I'm lucky—me

The daunting task of eating an elephant, armed w/ only a spoon

Some ppl can't handle the premium . . . they go for the regular

When you asked abt my father I couldn't bring myself to tell you that he died so I concocted stories abt him that got more & more fanciful until one day I said he's on a mission in space

心碎是我自導自演 . . . how do you like this self-guided performance?

Skinny-jeaned flirt: hey young & twitchy, I will gatecrash, be your earworm chorus, embrace your syncopated rhythms of funk

I am ready to accept whatever comes, so long as it is to my benefit. I am a truffle hog for excellence

Fiction writers love to look "furtively"

You always say nice things abt ppl. I perhaps say things harsher than I actually mean

Dems think that "if ur pro-life u should be pro-vaccine" is a sick burn

In British Hong Kong the most treasured housewarming gifts were Danish butter cookies in blue tins. These were, oddly enough, available from any of the pharmacies that dotted the island, the rough equivalent of Duane Reade or CVS. &, just as weirdly, it felt like the height of luxury. After the cookies were gone the tins would be used to stash sewing sundries & petty cash

The only time I ever attempted to shoplift I got caught but I was more concerned w/ hiding the fact that it was a pack of watermelon Bubblicious

Nothing good has ever followed a suggestion to play hide-n-seek

Can't really pay attention to space & light & galaxies & cosmos b/c I'm focused on shit happening right here

A low growl, blood pacts & wide-eyed wonder, let us be on the cusp. Loving me is good work if you can get it

I couldn't die w/o knowing your beautiful mind . . .

Some poems are abt the words . . .

Some poems are abt the symphony, how the sounds come together, the specific words aren't terribly important, it's a totality-of-the-circumstances sort of thing . . .

cf. those whose primary interest is in the actual words & not the images evoked

cf. those who are moved by the play of language

Orchestrated shiverings

Pushing the language beyond its basic signifying functions

A tension-filled balance

A graphic, painterly impulse

A lyric, musical impulse

Word combinations becoming strange presences like shifting registers in song

The plain-meaning, written word striking a nerve

Writers reworking passages so their prose works exactly the way they want it to . . .

Weaving these relationships & others into a shimmering narrative . . .

Sound leads to structure : Schönberg

Sound opens sound : Barbara Guest

The meaning lies in the sound

The meaning lies {   }

Action provoking feelings, the movement of soul

A critic said that Nabokov's feelings were like no one else's . . . really? No one else's?

Let's strive for fewer words & more feeling . . .

The feeling vs the image: "face down ass up"

CAVALLI LOUNGE LIZARD

in my delirium i thought abt all the war stories you never told me

i am better now

arranging hookups on yelp, smashing my pussy

chinatown a horrifically boring movie

i found veronica mars insufferable

don't pee on my leg & tell me it's raining

womxn love to touch your leg but maybe they just sense you need a hug

you are also hot

slick like mercury

small flame sweet swan

the quiz says i could be a wolf or a dolphin

purls before swine

mr bovary i insist on calling mr bowery & asking abt his highest floor

scroll thru nasa's fair-use images

book my seat for the rapture, business-class

pls do not congregate near the cockpit doors

THE COMPLETE HISTORY OF LOBSTER BISQUE

meditations on mini-golf, somewhere in pennsylvania

christian slater used to be cool but now hawks antivirus software

television is killing it
{ us }

marc jacobs botched his face-lift & somehow resembles galliano

my love, once saturated, is frail

my brother immigrated & turned into hamburger helper

i let bruce weber touch my junk, do his stupid breathing exercises

glitter & glue, a strict musk

i choose bbq paper based on how pink it is, ready for rimming

spend evenings convincing models they can be bartenders

if you had a time machine, would you go back & fuck paul ryan

the white house switchboard can connect you to anyone

cardinal richelieu praised my footwear

i said *prada, you may be familiar*

a disney prince paid me to write his papers

i argued for abolishing monarchies, sparking a constitutional crisis

whatever leo wants, leo getz

the talented cupbearer undid his jock, muttering abt his largesse

he had freakishly small hands, a wide stance

my silent admiration of a great cob, third leg a coney island special

my initiation proctor had majestic blue balls, a hubristic gape

my holes, the paddle

RASPUTIN

i may have a hog body but at least i'm a strong-willed pig [!!!!]

|

if u see someone w/ the exact same face kill them

|

for instance kirsten dunst

|

lube via lather—intimacy via stand-in—ice floe via polar bears

|

contused—confused [????]—how odd to see on the street—blossoming w/ neglect

|

they look like they'd rather be anywhere else [how i feel most days]

|

somewhere maybe in ohio [a funny word]

|

nobody "becomes" an alien [ur born dat way]

|

the darkest look [the wettest blade]

|

can't get it up [what is "it"] [lift it clean peachy flesh]

|

orange chicken [a kind of flagellation] [pinky in my slit u sample it]

|

sweet sausage [freak meat] [casual gait]

|

romney only prepared an acceptance speech [((inaudible))]

|

study his private his genital [jiffy lube] [we seethe]

|

sleepy b— fighting to stay awake [the phlebotomist] [so cute]

|

i'm a fluffer ur the star [ur fickle but i'm ur constant]

|

u like my loose morals & killer taste [for some reason daz important]

|

there is nothing that can get in the way of god's blessings [except irony]

|

most ppl don't read poetry—avoid being "most ppl" [drowned] [desperate]

|

when they elected me head boy i believe i misunderstood the requirements of the job

|

i just want to be slightly beautiful & lightly educated

|

up-&-coming [????]

|

no, i came [!!!!]

UNDERSTUDY

i don't have any rituals b/c i'm afraid of commitment

u confuse bts w/ btk

destined for breeding

i do most of my winning on my back

for days u babble on

for days my second mouth pretends to listen

touching u was like blotting out the sun

impossible to fathom until it actually happened

find me in the dark

thrumming w/ good fortune

no visitors w/o an appointment

everything abt u works & works in tandem

to seduce

i cannot countenance the disrespect of u not owning my books

clueless as a confederate

ditch me yellow american spirits

the capital, the provinces

not a dry eye in the room

TEACHER'S PET

like stephen hawking's oxford examiners

u know i am better than u

like the right to be forgotten

i can appreciate a good butcher stripe

i hate to put a label on the obvious

we don't want nobody nobody sent

as the disgraced model told the cop: *i'll suck your dick & balls if you let me go*

u need a masque to slough the ugly off

our eyes, flashing back & forth

i take care of u pasta salad

the stumbling block i look forward to

blow me, sam

i'm keeping my baby

feast ur eyes on this

FRIENDLY NEIGHBORHOOD
PHILOSOPHER-KING

*

Jump, he said.

The boy who spoke had nice eyes, hard yet soft like certain metals. Body lithe, like a dancer's, lean but powerful, erotic energy palpably coiled. Generally pleasant to be around, a steady presence, mostly just there, will remember your birthday. Don't confuse his shyness for timidity or a lack of ambition. The kind, if he gets his shit together, with the potential to go far.

The other, more-visibly-panicked boy, was plain, charming in the right setting, smarter than he looked. Most people are jealous phonies so they leap whenever someone real comes along, gravitating toward the simple-hearted and natural. Like him. Known for thoughts of a meandering sort, he was a hooligan-scholar with a slight lisp, capable of seeing beyond surfaces, sensing plots, always bypassing appearances, wanting to look under the hood of things.

He, too, had aspirations beyond being the boss's stooge, an unremarkable crony, and dreaded being stuck in middle management in perpetuity. Irony of ironies, it was perhaps this studiousness, this bias for rational analysis, that had so paralyzed him in life and career. In truth, he was the boss's translator, privy to many conversations of a highly-confidential nature, and could (till recently) be trusted to remain absolutely discreet. Or maybe he didn't know the value of the information he possessed and so couldn't capitalize on it. After all, some people don't know when they're sitting on a gold mine. In any case, he felt stuck in a rut, distressed day in and day out. The dazzle of something better, while very much an abstraction, was alluring and constantly looming. Something had to give.

*

Nobody intentionally goes into something knowing it's doomed for failure. When they started exchanging stories and plans for the future, they went through the usual will-he-or-won't-he, shit-what-have-I-done phases. Revealing yourself was tantamount to painting a bull's-eye on your back. Goodwill was rare in their line of work—trust being the thing that could get you killed or at least lose you a finger.

Then, one night, one of them (it wasn't clear which) took the other's hand, said they'd get through it together, and the deal was sealed. He admired the other's figure, muscly yet tragic, almost like they were from a different era . . . tufts of underarm hair like rust. He put his nose to it, unsure, then burrowed deeper. They fell into a joint swoon, precisely in tune, not minding the heat of the garage. The considerable, ever-present foot traffic lent a charge to the whole enterprise.

Soon they were thick as thieves, bonding over a shared love for drink and imported cigarettes. One was the type to hang up his shirt and fold his pants before sex; the other would patiently watch this ritual without complaint. They put foreign music on (usually jazz), playing cards, sharing dinner (typically fish). They lounged on white linen sheets, necks limp and bodies languid. They neglected their duties as much as possible, leaving coded messages for one another in chalk, marking the terracotta in their secret language. Their favorite color was cornflower blue.

Before long, though, their flirty sparring lost its luster, instead taking on a tedious sheen. Frustrations spilled over, hanging heavy. The precarity of their shared situation shortened fuses and drove them mad. Trouble beckoned.

*

Predictably, everything that could've gone wrong had gone wrong, Murphy's law and all that. They didn't anticipate the guards' schedule change, were surprised by another don visiting for an after-hours powwow (thus misjudging the number of men present), hadn't expected the catering van blocking their line of sight, their walkie-talkies cutting out, the damn medical bag not being sturdy enough, the body with the expression of bewildered terror, their (well-placed, they thought) decoy falling through . . .

Oh well, no time to dwell. He looked down at his partner, wincing, bracing himself. If he jumped and somehow survived, he'd remain a burden. They still needed to cross the expanse of the garden . . .

Any way you looked at it, he'd be the slower one, hobbled and risking their shot at escape. But he didn't have it in him to throw their painstaking plans away, wasting a summer's worth of work and condemning their future to a trash heap. Moreover, if he was being honest, he couldn't imagine the other with somebody else.

Some things you don't have to face—until you do. He blinked back tears, straining to see his partner. *I must love you if I let you this close*, he thought, overcome by an out-of-body serenity and calm. His partner, twisted face, alarming pallor, had by this point totally lost composure, a pathetic, sobbing mess.

He lowered his head, offering a small wave, wanting to mouth something, but it was too dark and too late and his partner wasn't in any state to catch on regardless. He started to raise his hands.

MY FOREVER PERSON

VOICE KINDA STRANGLED

I GUESS U HAD TO BE THERE

FOR SELFISH REASONS

STAR-SHAPED

IT'S EASIER, I THINK, TO SAY: *you make me want you, so you're manipulative*

ERGO ERGO ERGO

FREAKS TO THE FRONT

i can't remember how to write a good poem

heidegger says writing a poem is making a voyage of discovery

i don't know what a packrat is but i'd like to be one

look at this hymn to possibility

ur paper-tiger confidence

our fluctuations

their ongoingness

regrets, we have too many

insistent as the low rumble of a maserati

were u at dewey's coffee, admiring vanilla boys while waiting for ur vanilla drinks

sorry i was busy putting trash in my body

when i'm gone

will u be okay

or o.k.

or ok

POP SHOP II, 1988

The satisfying sound of the cologne cap snapping into place

The face shining with self-assurance

The emotional unavailability   The getting caught in the rain

The refusing to phone it in

The choosing without hesitation

The voice of naive bravado (the intimacy of it)

The renegade spider   formerly bright yellow   now glowing green

woke from a coma to find his favorite restaurant shuttered

By now the spider had learned the truth of his origins

The myth of his master being a physics professor was a lie

Wistfully the spider said   *we're a whisker away from being strangers*

You make me feel all the feelings   came the response

even the bad ones

At that the spider mounted him   (lo-o-o-ong legs)

& came in his head

& the newly-confident spider stepped into paradise

The masses wiped out

His prettiness undeniable

ST. MARK'S CONFESSIONAL

The notion of "poetic language" is bogus & elitist—everything is poetry

It looks like one of those creatures that's cute but could kill u

It's a golf pencil

It's a pair of cowboy boots

Look away!

Watch the gap!

Run for office?

Can I even run my own life?

I messed up

Give it to me straight

Our diet is longing

For mortals, nothing better

I'm contrite

Racecar

Sofa King

The other udders

Giving brain / skullfucking

Why not whisper it to me?

It's called quality assurance

MUSCLES

Person of good breeding: you're a dancer, always looking at your feet, studying your own form. You are monumental, already the best. The gift I can give you (let's be serious) is, I think, a sense of belonging. Someone who cares & consoles & celebrates with no expectation of return. You're soft & hard & smooth & rough. Your strength is magnificent like fog, like rain, like wind, precise as geometry, brutish yet tender. Don't know if you want me to go or tell you it's all right. I think I understand your tendency to retreat, your impulse to withhold, an *impulse* to not say anything (does that even square?). I've taken what little you've given me & cobbled together a sort of life. I'm capable of getting by, my existence a half-explored paradise, some vague satisfaction, a series of love letters to you, then a system of intelligent forgetting. You can't be resolved with reasoning, your own words killing any possibility of contentment. You don't believe in harmony, are done looking for it. We are green ghosts, delicate, dancing in our own air. We'll give it our all, get better together. The puppy-dog eyes, the shoulder squeeze, our madness.

明太子 MENTAIKO

the chinese character for "poetry" is the death of a party // how they changed the weather for the olympics // the ballpeen // bad head + a beef bowl // the word seminal makes me laugh // let the cum rest inside ur eyelids // forever starts when u stop caring // community is cute when u have nothing else // like the inside of a martian // rows of stuffed animals // move to england // make some tea // it's really going to happen soon // u didn't do anything wrong // not really // ashbery i like but u kinda have to read it in a haze // frank's cold-water flat let it wash over u // kleinzahler u don't even have to be sober // read it + watch mtv // poets love to tremble // murmur my 心路历程 // i just remembered a bad experience with someone named lavinia // it's really rude to ask someone *what do u feed that thing* // ur prodigious touching + tugging on his organism // some poems are just lists of fungi // u say *welfare* // i think milk subsidies // we neck // we fog // we furious // we contrail // fire up the cuisinart // a poetic resignation letter // release the hounds // we are lost bunnies // man ray's room service cart // liberace's valet // blackmailing everyone in the building // i want to attract crystals // lavender + blush + disgusting limoncello // wonton boys wanton emulsions // so much meat // every word of this is bullshit

EQUAL OR LESSER VALUE

title	length
you're a dynamo, a powerhouse	2:08
i ease the burden of your genius, take the edge off, make it bearable	2:14
i call you munchkin, call you donut, say *do you know munchkins are a kind of donut.* you look intently at me, reply *munchkins are midgets*	6:45
i let you pinch my lobster cheeks, wonder if you'll perform the same act of charity, let me know the one i'm seeing isn't good for me	3:19
you are magnet, we are flight controls, totally haywire	5:24
i want to let you happen to me, though i know what it means, two dogs regarding one another	0:47
open my eyes like voltaire, you know *george* magazine was named for george washington? how stupid is that	3:03
define "good" . . . define "skeeze"	0:06
bladderwrack, buckthorn & parsley seed aren't just the new pledges	6:04
a zamboni is not, in fact, flaky & delicious	5:53
imagine being a biden staffer & having to feign excitement for that mess	1:40
what's the most silent thing you've ever heard? why would you come to the city & be a nobody?	6:17
i suppose you could say we're the same, difference being i actually won	2:11
the republican senatorial campaign committee is responsible for the content of this advertising	0:19

SWIRLING HAUNTED HOUSE

we're living two lives
i have nothing to give but time

i always feel like you were just here
like you just left the room

i miss the nyu days
tireless, wallets fat with other ppl's money

bruce's hurricane fist
janet dancing on my tongue

my voice cracking like an eighth grader's
do our voices carry

we're in central park, drinking in the rain
spades or king's cup

drenched we hunt for a laundromat
freedom of movement is worthless with nowhere to go

loop of procrastinations
you tell me *you win some, you lose some, some get rained out*

when i care i hate myself (you)
even the biggest monsters have a weakness (you)

some of us would like to think this doesn't apply
let me destigmatize the animal

i know i am but what are you
i am a nice monster

i have a respectable occupation
not my fault you had a shitty childhood & no orthodontist

all health care, including dental, should be free
that's why i invented the little windows on packs of t-shirts

sure you can talk abt your friend
so glad we are strangers

endings are my favorite
the real suffering is getting there

HOMESCHOOL PROM KING

small house | only a few servants

boisterous bedroom | "chix" meaning chicken

bored with boys | lonely as it gets

crept into ur eyes | like it was prom night

journeys | they end the same

batman poster | crusty sock

(eatableass)

lovely | so gud

HAPPY WARRIOR

she fell off her scooter staring at me, determined as a drill bit

don't trust anyone who doesn't drink soda, we want lots & lots of pop

write poems in my head how other azns do math

u don't need my help dazzling coeds

my mouth pretty for when u come to town

so hot u cook an egg on it

so hot sunglasses come out all warped

so hot u get the chili pepper on ratemyprofessor

my mother knew better than to pretend-leave me someplace

i would've said *ok peace i'll let u know either way*

discerning as shibboleth, daylight savings can't buy shit

i hate that most memoirs are abt other ppl

see how they huddle, pretending to be something they're not . . . beefsteak tomatoes

unpitying boy im going to love u like sweet corn congee

teach u different ways to say *calves like cantaloupes*

make u mushroom soup from scratch

caress u furry creature

ditch our umbrellas in a rainstorm, get soaked like last week's dishes

dog & bone is a lazy name for a restaurant

try: rooster, reluctant poet & little halfwit who invented the universe

the same grave, the height of ridiculousness

ur lime jello, im fruit suspended in u

we hear the excited cries, think: he looks good out there

SIX BITS

1

interesting things found in backyards: pearls around a throat; california governor gavin newsom; the black bear reciting π to many decimal places; the feeble co-owner of wolf's furniture who's never met moonshine they didn't like; the gunrunner claiming that stars don't matter; the racist professor at montclair state refusing to return hr's calls; the bottle of l'eau d'hiver, designed by jean-claude ellena ("nose" at hermès), procured for an ex (very sad life, full of incidence, lost at sea)

2

my literary career began when i saw, on a flight bound for memphis, a boy read game of thrones. writing abt sex is hard to do. it comes off as too vanilla on the page: weirdness & a sense of wonder are important. there's always longing. make it linger. nowadays i refuse to be stuck reading apollinaire in a metal tube

3

sous la pluie
i love u all the way down
mouth full of spume, ur all egg & no sausage, that's how it goes, don't let me interrupt u
(i know u'll come slithering back the second i forget u)

4

in sleep i decorate u w/ garlands, part of ur symphony, reach out to u like an eternity, it's a matter, i think, of essential oils

5

patriotism, from a general vantage pt, a disease, like for-profit prisons (or, really, any prisons). loss, a little cave beguiling w/ its twists & turns, a private music, somewhat like doom, too much pity, joy ultimately illusive, sad (?) pathetic (?), i'd rather fall in a swimming pool than fall in love

6

u will crumble when u read my note
look closely if u want the truth
(yes u know) (how dare they)
when i feed on ur face this way

SYNTHETIC JUNGLE DIPTYCH

young cabbie w/ perfect recall

outdone by gps, rendered obsolete

i have accumulated a saeculum of useless knowledge

been disavowed like a burned spy

i imagine u basking, snarling

dumb as a peach

not in love w/ anyone, only fine fragrance left

no more body parts as commas, punctuation

tho fascinated by this spelling of "faeces"

payback for the restless nights wondering if u were doing ok

///

poster-pretty
  re-earning
admiration

— — —

ample charms
  prodigious
whispering

— — —

polite licks of ecstasy
  yes
pretty-as-all-get-out

— — —

love that's
  careless
wut stirs us

— — —

i will transmit
  to vladimir some handsome no-name
the one kissing me back

POEM BEGINNING WITH LINE FROM RILKE

Sometimes boys broke out of the mountains of childhood,

boyish error clinging like wet undershirts

we were on the elite bus, in comfortable shoes,

the more we talked the less credible we became

GLORIA VANDERBILT

I am: spokesperson for my race
Ur presence: enlarges all of space

Stupid boy: only ur fingers can fix me
Nesting so fat on spurious love: I hope u get stretchmarks

Ur sonar for Evanses: tangled suffering & tenderness
Two whiteboys huge as summer: gawking at u: momentarily consumed by private thoughts

One finally says: *I know u kiss boys*
U kiss his throat: nothing ticking in u but ████████

Geiger counter: haywire
Jealousy: atomic

The other declares: *these pieces aren't resonating w/ u*
U say: *iz a sweater*

U laugh when he breathes: *I wanna stretch u out*
Boondoggle swelling: pulsing w/ magnificent life

U say: *ur still reading One Hundred Years of Solitude*
But: *u smell like a party*

HALF-DAY CLOSING

attn poets: when do "fruits" stop "ripening"

like ashley benson's dealer

more green than the garden

so lemon-gold

i've read ur books, i like ur looks

u tout ur premium taste

garrulous love

precocious like apricot

a honey spell

lordy jacob elordi, lean as fillet

he took a shit while waiting for his test results

read rilke while lukas gage was rimmed on ep4 of white lotus

sampled wet soil after a parisien shower

le coeur n'est pas, seigneur, un don qui est rendu (time will tell)

DO U MIND WE ARE EATING HERE

Junipers In Rome
Flowers faded & shallow
Boys cast in a purple glow
Kinda gorgeous
The light, not the boys & their germs
Just kidding, the boys are uncommonly attractive
They have little tics that only come w/ knowing they're cute
Watching them, I think, counts as romance
Take me seriously
Unlike dick, poetry works better when ur drunk
My hard-on is very sincere
A high commissioner, even
Kofi Annan would take its calls
It would hear from confidential informant Bernie Bernstein w/o asking
Ppl used to eat cheeseburgers & fight to the death over Verlaine-branded nipple pasties
A lifetime supply of needs readily met
Like a chair w/ no seat
The problem w/ living alone is there's usually no one around to sit on ur face
I realize this
Like how I flirt w/ the girl when I really want the guy
I believe it's called a "honey pot"
Or "orange"
Thinking abt twunks & how they layer scent over scent instead of bathing
I think ur awful
Pls stumble home to me
I am

白球鞋 WHITE TENNIS SHOES

"poetry of the everyday" means boring poetry

foutez-moi la paix as in give me a break

u twirl the glass in ur hand, fingers deep inside

one sneakered foot perched on the other

sentences with no spaces

have designs on u

weather permitting, a/c on the beach

ppl write cronuts & frank ocean

i eat busily between ur legs

all-encompassing, so vantablack

i'm the best thing smoking thru ur life

a siren passing, there, then not there

i'm trying to fill my love empty

wink & a prayer

remember when kamala did an event with aka & her sorors went *skee-wee*

& a white reporter, not recognizing the calls, said they were hissing at her?

remind me what white reporters are qualified to write abt besides their too-big-to-fail?

immigrants never accidentally call their gf / teacher "mom"

are brazilian nuts from brazil?

no minor gods, ur major

i like how u take such good care of ur stuff

w/o u, no mathematics, no poetry

谢谢你·成为我的几分之几

DOING BATTLE WITH THE ONE WHO BRINGS FLOWERS

Sometimes[,] human

You, too, could write a poem

When I hold your watch up to my ear

the ticking makes me feel alive

Heading straight to the rosé aisle feels so revealing

I wake up thinking abt the novel *Push* by Sapphire & how she says "eyes slanted like Koreans"

Then laugh my way thru Valzhyna Mort's bison poem b/c of Cardi & "bison backs"

Sometimes I force myself to soften my gaze

look sympathetic like *I get you, young freak*

I go thru Mr. Slipper's text messages

text random numbers asking *who is this*

Among the tendrils under my pillow

A copper feeling

A buried heart

二三十 TWENTY, THIRTY

Et tu, Mojo Jojo

Among the tenements

we fight magic with magic

dodge hexes

mouth-to-mouth

The harbinger

The double cross

She moves on fast b/c her affections aren't worth much

Your affections are worth something if it takes a while to move on

No walks of shame

only parades of victory

Strange what you remember

The lilies

A clap of thunder

TOO GOOD FOR YOU & OTHER STORIES

too old to be a wunderkind. too cute to be a golem

i staged my bedroom to look like yours—more comfortable when we make babies

come feed me with your fingers. most men can't see past the curls

god's plan a dog's breakfast—is it not in your service that i codeswitch from brilliant to genius

don't be a drag. ride me like a rickshaw

_____ is boring. she has a flash of insight once every 40 years

having received visual confirmation. this proof of life

you put out. tell him you're horny in a stage whisper

once you've dispensed with—disposed of—the operative

you're ready for the seafood special. that afternoon d-lite

54

you nitpick. look for bones in egg whites. i wanna hang out with you & your rainbow slides

poets love segments & orange anything—john's sucking & fucking—now i have a bone to pick

it isn't distracting if romance is the goal (romance should always be the goal)

wait for a sign. so big & ballsy

☺ ☺ ☺

ANTISOCIAL SOCIAL CLUB

banish the word "offering"—i prefer payment

ur likes are insincere

at dream state university

guests may enjoy warm seltzer

hollow skies

my soiled vuitton panties

it's a family affair

i love appearing as epigraphs in ur messy poems

this may surprise u but i was horrible at woodshop

sometimes i feel like a gorilla in an elevator

<u>dream:</u> greg is not getting any younger. i ask when he'll put that lovin' on me

thankfully i'm walt's type

bianca jagger—i can't believe i said u were cute & u said *noted for the future*

the problem with pretending u have no feelings?—it catches up to u

NEXT ON THE UPGRADE LIST

the town, found

watching the clock, no chance of meeting the stork

u louse, irascible, waffle-cone sweet

read dead ppl, say keats like "kates" b/c representation

the lee daniels casting couch, skin-to-skin contact

cute by acclamation, ignorance of jude law is no excuse

preference for harsh lighting, total glutton for punishment

campus sbarro—loving u is a losing game

the lofty confusion of a final journey

acolytes scurrying

moles back underground

an instinct, a deathwish

striking & striking

till unbearably soft

ZUM ZUM

bullshit artist with the perfect spin

tell them you're not that innocent

i'm running counterintelligence

earmark: $3.2 million for researching the genetics of harbor seals

crabs cool to the touch

aching to be fucked

you could perhaps be sipping tequilas sunrise with a republican of color

you could be the tom daley to their dustin lance black

why does the fridge have a "vacation" setting

when my meat never rests

to think of you alone

touching yourself like a piggy

MY MOTHER SAID I'M TOO ROMANTIC

They say you become what you most desire

Which explains these salmon shorts

My legs stubs of radish

Some poets are horrible at email—others are just horrible

My clients—coplaintiffs red-tailed hawk, red-winged blackbird, heart-shaped leaves, hare's fur, assorted arroyo & bougainvillea—are suing poet Arthur Sze for inappropriately profiting off their names, images & likenesses

Our shared bunnyhood, bodies great & glistening

I would like it if I was shat out by you—you do that shit

Your jets of white

Bubbles smuggled in your love sacs

Cream of the unrequited variety

You go thru ppl like Kim Jong-un goes thru courtesans—used, then ousted!!!!

You reached into my pants & took what you wanted

Your racist bone in my body

I must leave you—I have received a text from my best friend—DoorDash

LEG OF LAMB

Remember when the GOP did an autopsy to find out why they were losing elections

Turns out ppl hate them & ppl hate their policies

Nobody ever chooses Pepsi, unexciting hotel art (sorry)

The Kyoto Protocol, painstaking abt my sexual habits / mores

Robes of gold & green, Trojans at the student union

Where is he, overwhelmed (!) by the dramatic window

Have I missed him sufficiently

Is that enough to impress, how much I've missed him

We danced together like little superstitions

A passing fancy, mouse-in-a-hat absurdity

He saw clean thru me, audacious & practiced

The world a mess, his hair perfect

A plea & a challenge, something abt a palm tree

I have truly said too much

GIN & MILK

in canada the drinking age varies across provinces & territories; could u Imagine not caring across provinces?; exactement; nubile wunderkammer; package of sex overflowing at the front; pulverize me; detach from me only after u have come; i reveal too much to u; r u a witch; u think i am obsessive monster; i obsess over ur moons; ur rich semen; ur warpath, ur fabled instruments of destruction; ur wit, ur abundance; some foreign attachment; emerging from behind a zipper; w/o so much as a sigh; it is true obscenity; the tie-dyed terry cloth hugging his cock; thru the fabric looking like a hose; drinking him, devouring his progeny; the air is murderous; sometimes, when ur given a sign, it's ur obligation to recognize it; to act on it; there is nothing i am looking forward to but going to the cheese shop; in total obscurity; swallowed by cheeses; the pungent smells; i can accept it but i wouldn't say that i'm fine with it; what could be sadder than toting a bag of salad; acquitted; my dignity remains intact

COCO CHANEL SEARCH & RESCUE

this reciprocal torture

this 互相傷害

you treasure, smithsonian-grade

bird brain

if you have this idea, i can, too

our sameness led us to fight, leads to these rows

slurp you like noodle, nothing you don't already know

you are a task, one requiring intense concentration but bringing immediate relief

like pulling a splinter from a paw

you keep asking what i want but your two heads are distracting

a contract is an offer & an acceptance

i can almost believe it

more rough, more sorry

you broke it

冷战 COLD WAR

I dream that Rumsfeld says "that's all" to me & return to my desk, sulking

I wake up to find a female ghost on my chest, adamant abt popping a squat. I call out for my personal Jesus

I wake up next to a cheesesteak. They leave

Self-care is exhausting. I need to be taken care of

Most days I put on a good face, a werewolf

Moment of weakness: slip under a friend's tongue, liking it

Surprisingly pamplemousse, suddenly Domingo

The last time I see Mathias is in Tribeca. He fights w/ his girlfriend over me

One day I will learn to stare w/o longing

A lot can happen in a month

Disavow me daddy

This poet has no intention

I'm living out the logical conclusion of Meet the Fockers

Your mouth reminds me of goodbye

STUDENT-ATHLETE'S
COLLEGE RECRUITMENT GUIDE

lance: buyer of track pants & athletic socks

perfect loved boy give me a future

i like ur boy traits: ur too-thick ache's elations

we can look at some terrifying art inside my mouth

young boy enters a dancehall feet loose

he fixes cocktails blindfolded

runs down the wooden escalator *clack clack clack*

david archuleta lookalike stares the whole night

why do i read the right-hand side first

is it my chinese dna

if i am responsible

it is for everything

hardy explorers on borrowed time

ur dukedom with fairy lights

the mother of all orgasms

still unsure how we were led astray

is it possible i prefer ur breath over mine

nuance is poisonous

let's talk generalities

res ipsa loquitur: the thing speaks for itself

[comments turned off]

U.F.O. & DOLPHIN, 1982

The United States ~~is no longer~~ a nation of empathy.
                    { was never }

{ seriously, tho, you're on your own, tho, circling the drain, brah }

* * * From January 2010 to July 2019, at least 90 ppl were murdered & likely many more injured, during encounters with US border agents. In June 2010, 15-year-old Sergio Hernández was playing on the Mexican side of the US-Mexico border when a US Border Patrol agent, Jesus Mesa, fired shots across the border, hitting Hernández in the face & killing him.

* * * While at play, Hernández was standing on the Mexican side of a culvert that marks the boundary between Ciudad Juárez, Mexico, & El Paso, Texas. Mesa claimed to be engaged in his law enforcement duties when a group of young men began throwing rocks at him from the Mexican side of the border.

* * * The Hernández family filed suit in US federal court, seeking to hold Mesa responsible for their son's death, but the Supreme Court, by a 5-4 vote, ultimately ruled that the lawsuit could not go forward. The Court concluded that Congress, rather than the courts, should decide whether to allow plaintiffs to seek money damages from a federal official.

* * * The Hernández family contended that Mesa had used excessive force against their son, violating the boy's rights under the Fourth & Fifth Amendments to the Constitution. The family pointed to a 1971 case, *Bivens v. Six Unknown Named Agents*, in which the Supreme Court allowed a lawsuit seeking money damages from federal officials for violating the Constitution to go forward. But in 2017, after hearing oral argument in the Hernández family's case for the first time, the Supreme Court sent the case back to the lower courts for them to consider the Court's decision in *Ziglar v. Abbasi*, holding that a *Bivens* remedy should not be extended to a "new context" when there are "special factors counseling hesitation" & Congress has not affirmatively authorized a suit for damages. When the case went back to the Court

of Appeals, that court concluded that the Hernández family could not bring a *Bivens* claim against Mesa. The Supreme Court concurred.

* * * This is, of course, lacking, as Justice Kagan appeared to suggest during oral argument, positing:

Why wouldn't the United States say, you know, we live in a country in which courts play an important role in determining whether conduct is lawful. And that's not an embarrassment to the United States or the executive branch.

///

When courts rule in a limited way, we say they do so "narrowly" — usually meaning the plaintiff in a particular case will come out disappointed (& sometimes screwed). We also say that the court's decision is "confined to" *x* or *y*, which generally means that a future case must be very factually similar ("on all fours") in order for a claim to be "cognizable" . . . an example of such a formulation would be this: x *newly-recognized right or cause of action shall only apply to plaintiff-Batmans who have also appeared in the television series* ER . . .

Do you see how narrowly these things can be drawn? It has been 40 years since the Supreme Court has recognized a new *Bivens* remedy; in other words, in the nearly 50 years since *Bivens*, the Court has only extended it twice.

As a ppl, we have a reputation for rushing to the courthouse to redress any slight (real or perceived). But for such a litigious country, it is actually very difficult to sue certain parties or pursue some kinds of cases. Suing the state, for example. Or law enforcement. The rationale for effectively blocking such cases ranges from:

—"judicial economy" (an objectionable & meaningless theory cut from whole cloth, meaning *don't clog up our dockets*) to

—"separation of powers" (meaning the other branches can do most things unfettered unless the actions are truly egregious — or, God forbid, regulate the courts, in which case they will step in!) to

—"national security considerations" (*this country's border-control policies are of crucial importance to the national security of the United States* . . .) to

—"the conduct of foreign policy or diplomatic concerns" (*the US government is always responsible to foreign sovereigns when federal officials injure foreign citizens on foreign soil . . .*) to

—"operational considerations" (*implying that a private right of action for damages in this transnational context increases the likelihood that Border Patrol agents will hesitate in making split-second decisions . . .*) to

—an unstated & suspect need to protect the privileged positions of particular individuals or entities

—the list goes on . . .

///

Instead of speculating abt the (strong) likelihood of law enforcement officers making bad decisions in the future, we should be focusing on bad decisions *we know they have already made.*

Given the result in this case, similar incidents will continue if law enforcement officers cannot be held accountable in civil suits. The unlikely prospect of discipline or criminal prosecution will never provide a meaningful deterrent to abuse at the border or elsewhere.

Rogue officer conduct falls within an all-too-familiar, definitely not a "new," *Bivens* setting. Courts should be much less willing to cabin doctrines & undermine essential rights foundations: as is true in other contexts, maintaining the status quo usually means the little guy gets shafted.

If anything, we should be making it easier for ppl to seek justice, to test their legal theories before the courts, to have the imprimatur of the court to access the kind of serious fact-finding often blocked by reluctant or recalcitrant parties who want to call your bluff.

Our courts should be a sympathetic forum for everyone—the aggrieved, of course, but especially our most vulnerable, ppl with no one else to turn to & nowhere else to go. Our condolences to the Hernández family.

THE OVERLY AGGRESSIVE FORTUNE COOKIE SPEAKS

{ yikes hope you avoided the scallops }

{ that bag is fake }

{ great jewellery why you live in squalor }

{ only white ppl can afford language poetry }

{ spam not good for your bloat }

{ you stuff like rangoon }

{ don't read this while you cross street }

{ what came first chicken or egg foo young }

{ too much call of duty bad for you }

{ i introduce you rigor mortis }

{ i'm not wearing anything }

{ this is cheap date }

{ he break up b/c you tedious }

{ mp means merchant's price }

{ yellow ranger was yellow }

{ you look triceratops }

{ you tourist on stolen land }

{ immigration big problem }

{ existing aint shit }

{ not now not again not ever }

{ i'm not bitter you're just guilty }

{ blake is the one }

{ shit just go }

不适合 NOT SUITABLE

i don't wanna read abt tongues unless they're on me

u cling to me like religion

this exciting prospect

that stranglehold of infatuation

desire is the birthplace of prophets

sympathy is cheap but longing costs (no afterglow)

we're extremely eloquent therefore extremely dangerous

extremely online chrissy teigen would tell her to take a dirt nap

u pressed to my cold lips

no chance to slip by unnoticed

no time to seek out the others

we throw caution to the wind

we are bent!

ur biology the subject of so many thoughts

it has me restless

did that photo awaken something in u

u can be honest with me, practice ur water sports

i could put it in my horlicks

a _____ who isn't interrupted is stunned into silence

we dissolve into puddles of slobber

ur too cute

nobody would ever wanna disappoint u

love is kinda terrible

LIFE IS GOLDEN

on the hottest day of the year

the back of his neck slick with sweat

i wondered abt his collar size

admired his swimmer's build

his getting-pudgy sitcom-dad face

i like them a little pudgy

their bodies starting to give in to aging

we discuss community so we feel less lonely

talk abt our depravity

how you make my sheets smell amazing

we patter on abt bars & cruising & safe spaces & swish—

debating what archetypes we fit & how convincingly

our prurient interests provoke contemporary standards

we say *beast!* at the bridge-&-tunnel crew walking by

never admitting how you make me a better person

(only old-timers do that)

our attentions drift like fog

at a couple we shout *ditch the giraffe!*

i inhale the smaller boy

take in legs lean & shapely

feel the sourness assault my nostrils

like meat left out too long

in the village where the sodomites gather

SUEDE KISSES

help!   i won't be your kitty genovese   if i scream you better come

white womxn will tell you abt their vacations   but mostly wanna call the cops

fingers ready to dial   i won't be your kitty dukakis   you cry for me

you put them down   half moon bay   the sandworms are starving

          we like that sun-bleached senseless death

where were you last tuesday   had a good line abt getting fucked & getting fucked over

you cumstain i've lost it now   i'll get you back   why don't you reach around

          sensitive whiteboy   aggressively normal   so pale he's glowing

planned his life around hope hicks & her lies   has a separate computer for porn

i saved him from one bad marriage   a move to miami   it's not sleep that helps me get over it

i just have terrible recall   daniel!   you with the jug ears & full lips don't ask me for ten dollars   rookie

pretty face   mole on nipple   indeterminate sexuality   so sweet & wild

spray your nocturnal fragrance   you're the only one in my bed

you on my loveboat   you in my band

so many pointless ballads   no way to make them dance

longing for my rosebud   the bridges i burn lighting the way

sonia says no relationships   until you give birth to yourself

no passion   no kidding around   no jingle jangle

sonia is wrong   the program's produced its share of stars   three cats

two sets of twins   a psychagogue grandma stunning her attacker   with flowers

m*n are lonely & would be happier with an 8-inch dick   this wisdom murmured into your bulge

you tense!   horny underneath!   i am sympathetic

UPON HEARING SYLVESTER FOR THE FIRST TIME

Edmund White describes '70s San Francisco as a "gay finishing school" but everyone knows finishing schools are already gay

It's certainly true that for a period of time New Yorkers only wore black. This has since changed, with the infusion of frat boys & their straight-boy babble

Remember that time we went out & I smoked all your cigarettes? Haha pussy

Context cues are important in language. Suppose I told you we hired feluccas to go across the Nile. Given that context, you'd probably (correctly) guess that feluccas were boats of some sort. But context is only helpful some of the time, b/c you never tell me anything, you have a whole life w/o me & you're impossible to figure out

Jealousy isn't futile; jealousy is an engine

Speaking of futility, when that muppet de Blasio ran for president, his slogan was "con don" w/o realizing, of course, that it's Spanish for *condom*

What's "international cuisine"? She generally served risotto with spring vegetables & always ended with a sundae cart, an idea she stole from American Airlines. The best policy was to get a sundae with everything on it. This guaranteed an approving look from the hostess

I loved the whole scene, your expensive father delivering a lush speech, after which he's ruminating, thinking of "business machines" & chasing down taxis & home ownership (forget affordability), definitely something from a different era, wholly outside the realm of possibility

It's a generational thing, dudes who'd rather stand in the rain than go in a bookstore, whiteboy-sensitive, tempers flaring with unqualified enthusiasm, at the alehouse hoping for skin & awaiting ruin, Gods & vampires, two made-up things (*wait, don't you think vampires are real?*), yes, lead me away from the bar, we want the same thing, sweet relief, a sympathetic ear

Boys holding hands & ducking into 45 Orchard, complexions like cereal milk, maybe they sense us staring (but who isn't), one with a little hunchback, so slim it's sickening, making us go *awww young love, just you wait*

That talky, revelatory poetry, no one more anonymous than poets, I know the signs, be bathroom for me, we'll stop at nothing, tant pis pour eux!

MAX'S KANSAS CITY

humbly, i recognize, my heart's weak as a victorian's, but it's glowing, we're a freedom-loving ppl, us, sighs breaking from u, rather innocent, my mouth opening, truth rattling in my throat, what to do with our seven minutes in heaven?, did i lock the door? did i leave the oven on? do i own an oven?, look at me, total amateur, turning so quickly, i twist the light, trip over errant wires, u catch me, stroke my hair, i stretch up to u, we clasp, passion rendered exquisitely, touch so much we learn the sublime, give it a new name, ur handsome & powerful & can throw me abt, u sniffle, i hate malls, malls are scenes of violence, let's stay here till closing, but before u go, update ur will, if cash-poor, no poems, art ok

ACCIDENTAL ANARCHIST

(we could live between two parentheses)
says the chinese poet

it's me
the chinese poet is me

i go by many names
poet-saint

friendly neighborhood
philosopher-king

yes!! daddy
i see u when i close my eyes

enraptured, alert, waiting for ur number to be called
no sluggish listening here, no siree

at the movies i saw russell brand sit on a stranger's lap
i guess if ur famous they really let u do anything

the placid sun asks where u at how u doing
the seashells approach a jackal

leopards defy language
parrots are rough trade

we the last of the small-town playboys
reputations in tatters

u the alchemist
i the historian

take deadwood
the lust of libertines

deposed princes
chiselled pretenders

make dutiful robots
weighing no more than breath

long hair crying out for a paring back, a pruning
i don't like u with downturned mouth

u my waterloo
has anyone ever told u sorrel filly not aquatic

enjoying his company
a sort of sly intimacy never discussed

a great surf breaking
washing over u like well-earned praise

convoke a crew
see the shape of things that never came

still somehow
kind of bobbing along

a practical compromise:
rattan chairs, highball glasses & foam

whiff of landed gentry
amiable, gentlemanly

quiet, comfortable familiarity
dunhill lighter clicking shut

u tore such happiness from him
unforgivable, welcome as a gash in the throat

suppress these greedy, suspicious urges
a fascination that persists

desire as a birthright
offended & fearful

the light-eyed dandelion boy shivers theatrically
plainly nourished

memories are like cells ; ; ; ; ; ;
always replaced by new ones

FREE THROW

So glad you could make it

said no one ever

You thirsty for Zac's hairy chest

Big booty mouthfuls of it

Miles & miles of perfect skin

You rub one out for Orin

When they come for you

just say you don't care

CHARLATANS

guy fawkes night

we brace for quiet

i hate u the least

statement of our life

virgin words like nintendo

the emily rat

pitiful bbq chicken, masses & masses

stripped of color

& in between

so many dates u always come with soundbites

for u two can be a cluster

ur luscious grapes

hefty & dewy

the head, like clay

SIMPATICO

—7 nights a week ? every line a mic drop ? feels like groundhog day—

—sad bunny bathed in blue light—

    —i believe it was gandhi who said *i'll be nicer if u'll be smarter*—

—why do ppl say *towheaded* when they mean something else—

—i never say *suck my dick* b/c ppl will say ok—

    —in some countries this passes for food—

—new love ? no such thing—

—fondling the troops ? uselessly m.i.a.—

    —naked sunlight ? imagined openness—

—stop counting ? i'm not 14 lines—

—both ? neither—

    —who taught u the most (abt love)—

—if yvor winters can rhyme "lust" w/ "dust" ur probably doing ok—

    —god knows what i'd be w/o u ? very odd ? in retrospect—

—we've seen some things ? too bad no one asked why u cry so much—

JACKET REQUIRED

dear evel knievel: ur a wreck

dear messenger: i shoot u now

i have many friends who are white allies

in much of asia, white is a funereal color

the phantom—the silver fern

some (a lot) of this shit i can't even pretend to care abt

the weirdest hillary factoid is how she carries hot sauce in her armani purse

u want peanut sauce wit them pawn crackers

my overcaffeinated ass

m*n can also be scientists

today is friday

no more "but the feeling"-type stuff!! nonsense!! says nothing!!

i was wit a chick & a bunch of bros told me *u can do much better*

!! (i assume meaning them)

if i say their vision for the country is cataracts, is that politically correct?? do we care??

wut are some words we can borrow from the other side?? cuck?? snowflake??

every day a new mood

ur lower mouth—ur inside job

go to ur mudflap gurls—they look spaced out

u compete in ur own division

are u as lovely as u look

!! (this is the writing u've been waiting for)

wut wow it really is u

伊斯坦堡 ISTANBUL

\

it was a kind of seeing . . . a roiling . . . oocupying & arousing

 this surprising glut of poems abt googling ppl with the same name . . .

 who cares . . . unless it's francis bacon . . . or michael chang

  ur zoned for excellence

\

nothing compares to u . . . ur miyagi-do *&* cobra kai

 ur cognac cherries . . . so much brilliance contained in one little package

  in prep . . . 3 colors is a rainbow

\

ur a good problem to have

 i always watch the parodies first

  like liquor before beer . . . we have the power to change things

\

suddenly bewildered by love . . . can something be shocking *&* tasteful at the same time

 ur amazing adventures . . . i am humble footnote

  plastic umbrellas . . . lungs full of glass

words cloaking themselves . . . betrayal pouring out of u

nothing ever stays between my fingers

trust . . . one day we will forget it all

WORKING STIFF

funny u seem inconsolable

u look like something i wish i loved more

pale apples

handsome piece of maple

lit randomly by dew

keep ur sweet marrow, i'm vegan

like peggy g. said

i'm not an art collector

i'm a museum

the last thing u see

fit into my crabhole

that dick, all at once

high as u can reach

will that be everything

ACKNOWLEDGMENTS

With thanks to:

Elias Baez . . .

Zach Issenberg—hi, Eric :) . . .

Max Kruger-Dull . . .

Jason Zuzga . . .

My beloved blurbers, for their unimpeachable judgment . . .

Emily Mahon, for the beautiful cover art, which is like nothing else out there . . .

Marisa Siegel, Maia Rigas, Olivia Aguilar & the entire NUP team, for supporting this project & believing in it from the very beginning . . .

The editors at *Another New Calligraphy/Impossible Task*, *Barzakh*, the *Boiler*, the *Cincinnati Review*, *Fence*, *Moon City Review*, *New Delta Review*, *No Contact Mag*, *Nowhere Mag*, the *Rumpus* & the *South Dakota Review*, for their early support . . .

& as always, YOU~